purposed

A Highly Favoured Life Teen Devotional

VOLUME I

1st Edition published in 2023
2nd Edition published in 2025

ISBN:
978-1-967189-10-6 (paperback)
978-1-967189-11-3 (hardback)

Table of Contents

Introduction

What are you going to do when you graduate from high school? When will I find my Prince Charming? Will I still have my besties in my life when we move on after school? Will I attend college? What summer job should I apply for?

Daily, you are hit with the questions of your future. The devil tries to overwhelm your mind with the "what ifs" of life. He seeks to distract you from what matters with petty locker room dramas. Satan wants to turn your gaze on the cute guy across the room instead of preparing for real marriage.

The devil uses so many tactics to pull you away from what is really important - growing in your walk with the Lord and seeking to please Him with your life. This time probably seems like a whirlwind. You have new emotions, new friends, new ideas, new experiences, etc. None of these things are wrong! But if you are not careful, you will let your mind and heart become filled with the nonessential.

This devotional was written by godly adult ladies for the purpose of encouraging you to take this time to grow. Do not waste one moment of your teen years distracted by the world. Keep your focus on Christ!

He will never disappoint. "Keep thy heart with all diligence; for out of it are the issues of life," Proverbs 4:23. Protect your heart. Purpose today to keep Him always first in your life.

Develop a Skill

By Hannah Kasprzyk

Then answered one of the servants, and said, Behold, I have seen a son of Jesse the Bethlehemite, that is cunning in playing, and a mighty valiant man, and a man of war, and prudent in matters, and a comely person, and the LORD is with him.

I Samuel 16:18

What a glowing recommendation David received from this servant! I can assure you David did not become any of the things the servant mentioned just by chance. As a shepherd, David probably spent many a day out in the fields playing his harp, practicing with his sling, and spending time with God. Because of this, God was able to use David in amazing ways as a warrior, Israel's king, a songwriter, and as an example for generations as "a man after God's own heart."

God has given each of us a unique set of talents and abilities. What are yours? If you don't know, take time to discover what it is you are good at. Maybe God has gifted you in sports, music, understanding languages, crafts/DIY, baking, working with children, or writing (just to list a few). Wherever your talents lie, put the time and effort into becoming the best at it that you can be. As you determine your abilities, be careful that you do not fall into the deadly trap of comparing yourself to the abilities of others! God tells us in II Corinthians 10:12 that this is not wise.

Be content with being the person God made you and focus on becoming the person God wants you to be. In John 21:22, Jesus reminded Peter that what God does with another person's life has no bearing on what God wants for you.

As you develop your talents, keep in mind the purpose ought to be to be used by God. God certainly wants to use you! Your talents were not given to you for you to keep to yourself. God gifted you with certain abilities so that He can use you to serve Him in special ways. Use that foreign language out soul winning, use your musical talent in church, help coach that junior varsity team, work in a children's ministry, write stories and encouraging blogs, bake treats for the shut-ins or church fellowships, or help with the crafts and decorations for church events. You never know how the talents you develop today can be used by God, both now and in the future. Keep your eye out for opportunities to be involved and use your talents for God.

Too often, teenagers can make the mistake of wasting their teenage years with the thought, "I'll get to that when I'm older." How many opportunities and even blessings could you forfeit with that kind of mindset? Preparation needs to happen now so that whenever God opens a door, you are ready to walk through it. Being ready doesn't happen by accident, and it does not happen overnight. As you get older, God will give you even greater opportunities for service and be able to greatly use you.

Challenge: What skills do you have? What opportunities to serve has God given you? Start developing yourself today and watch as God uses you in ways beyond your wildest dreams!

purposed

Notes:

Prayers

When Dreams Turn to Disappointment

By Rachel Post

---

*Even the youths shall faint and be weary, and the young men shall utterly fall:
But they that wait upon the LORD shall renew their strength; they shall
mount up with wings as eagles; they shall run and not be weary;
and they shall walk, and not faint.*

Isaiah 40:30-31

This passage is so powerful, especially in your life. The everlasting God and Creator of the earth is looking to give you the power to overcome. Wow!

As teenagers, we often think our life is secure. We think that what we expect to happen, will indeed happen. We plan for the next teen activity or conference, we plan for the next volleyball game or school trip, and we plan to hang out with our friends after school and to see them again in the next school year. These things seem guaranteed.

For some, it works out this way, and they go through their teenage years living out the predictable. For others, it doesn't work that way. Well, why is that? That doesn't seem very fair. You are right!

The everlasting God is looking to give you the power to overcome.

It is not fair, but did God ever promise "fair"? No. He promised to give us the power and strength that we need to persevere through the unexpected.

I found myself in this position the summer before my senior year of high school. I was set to be captain of the cheer squad and co-captain of the volleyball team. I had amazing friends, loved my school, and lived for annual teen camps and youth conferences. I was blissfully unaware that life can change in the blink of an eye. My perfect little "Baptist bubble" would soon pop, and it would shake my idealistic view of life.

Unforeseen circumstances came like a thief in the night and snatched away my dream "senior year." Just like that, everything I knew was taken away. It felt as if my life was crumbling right before my eyes. Why me? Why now? Wasn't I the "good Christian girl" who deserved the "perfect" senior year? Why should someone else's decision have such a negative influence on my plans?! It just wasn't fair! ... And I was right, it wasn't fair, but it was life.

God didn't give me the picture-perfect end to my high school career that I thought I needed or deserved. Instead, we moved to another state, and I sat in my living room doing school on my laptop. No, it wasn't what I wanted, but God was more real to me during that situation than He had been when I was in my cushy, Christian school environment. I saw firsthand that God does not use only teen leaders and pastors to speak to us. For the first time in my life, I saw Him use the Bible to comfort me and bring me peace amid a very unpeaceful year. He grew my faith and reliance on Him in ways that would have never been possible had I not been shaken up. Even though I was weary and fainting, He upheld me. He never grew tired. He never wavered. The Creator of the world renewed my shortage of faith, replenished my strength, and helped me to mount up with wings as eagles.

Dear teenager, I know that when plans change and the unexpected happens, it seems as though the Lord has left you. But it is quite the opposite. He has never been so close. He has never been so eager to give you the necessary power to overcome. He is right there in your discouraged Bible reading and your sorrowful prayers. He is never weary of you.

Challenge: What disappointments are you facing right now? Read Isaiah 40:28-31. I encourage you today to look for Him amidst the rubble. You will find Him.

purposed

Notes:

Prayers

Ropes That Catch and Hold

By Nicole Redmon

Jesus answered them, Verily, verily, I say unto you,
Whosoever committeth sin is the servant of sin.

John 8:34

Sin can have such a grip on us. Sometimes the grip is so delicate that we may not even feel the tightening that is taking place. Sin truly can be a rope that catches and then holds us in place. The more we try to wiggle our way out of it, the more entangled we get. Never underestimate the power of sin to make you a slave.

Do you ever look at one of your friends whom you know is living in open sin and think to yourself, "Poor girl, she is just ruining her life." We shake our heads and go on about our merry way. But what we should be doing is being spiritually aware of our own sin. We may not be living in open sin like our friend, but we sure can harbor some sinful behaviors that are not seen on the outside but take hold deep down on the inside. Don't kid yourselves, ladies. Sin is clever!

Pride is not always easy to spot in our lives. Proverbs 16:5 says, "Every one that is proud in heart is an abomination to the LORD: though hand join in hand, he shall not be unpunished." The Lord sees that pride that you think is tucked away. Be careful! God gives us a great warning concerning the dangers of being prideful. Proverbs 16:18, "Pride goeth before destruction, and an haughty spirit before a fall." Remember Romans 3:23: "For all have sinned, and come short of the glory of God." Nobody is perfect.

The hidden sin of resentment alone will captivate your thoughts. It can take over in a heartbeat and choke you to the point where there is hardly any life left in you. You can get so resentful that all you seem to do is relive the same hurt over and over. You are a slave to that sin of resentment. It has caught you and now has a hold on you. It will not let go either, because sin's grip is so tight.

We have got to cut the ropes! I John 1:9, "If we confess our sins, he is faithful and just to forgive us our sins, and to cleanse us from all unrighteousness." By the power of God's amazing grace, you can cut those ropes that have caught you and are holding you captive.

Challenge: Ask the Lord to forgive you of those sins that are keeping you a slave. Be determined not to entangle yourself in those ropes of sin that can and will catch and hold you hostage. If you do not know how to take those first steps to cut the ropes of sin, talk to your parents or godly influences in your church (pastor's wife, Sunday school teacher, youth pastor's wife, etc.).

purposed

Notes:

Prayers

The Key to Finding Missing Things

By Alyssa Schutt

If thou seekest her as silver, And searchest for her as for hid treasures;

Proverbs 2:4

What does it take for you to find something? Maybe you are looking for your phone or keys or cup of coffee or your bag that you need for work or school. Maybe you are looking for a certain store or coffee shop that you've been wanting to go to. You might be looking for a friend or family member in a store or a room and start calling their name. Or, the worst one yet, you are trying to feel for that one outlet behind your bed to charge your phone at night. What tools do you use to find these things or people? Your voice? Your eyes? Your hands? Your nose (to find that freshly brewed coffee)? Maybe even your map on your phone?

Whatever you are trying to find, you must use something of yourself to find it. We find things through this word – diligence. You are looking for that missing object with diligence because you know you need it. This same diligence is what it takes to attain knowledge and wisdom from God.

Open your Bible and take a look at Proverbs 2:1-9. I'll meet you back here when you're ready.

Let's zero in on verses 1-4. In your Bible, or separately in your journal, take a few moments and underline or write each action verb that you would need in order to find a missing object.

Receive. Incline. Apply. Criest [cry out/call]. Liftest up thy voice. Seekest. Searchest. These are the words we use to find things! We receive words – we cry out and lift up our voice to find someone. We seek and search for that object we need. All of these actions require an amount of diligence. If we go back to the thought of trying to find something: we flip over everything, checking and rechecking places where we felt we might have left it. We ask everyone we see if they have seen it and look if they can help us find it. Again, you are looking for that missing object with diligence because you know you need it.

Have you ever looked for something without diligence? In about two minutes flat, you are moving on to the next thing in your day because you are already tired of looking for that object. It loses importance. Don't let your relationship with Christ lose importance. Keep that tenacity!

This same diligence is what it takes to attain knowledge and wisdom from God. So, I encourage you, sister, to dig in. Dig into your Bible. Start with what you know. And, for the things you don't know, ask God to show you or ask a spiritual mentor. Find connections with people who have diligence in their relationship with Christ. Understanding the fear of the Lord and finding the knowledge of God can be overwhelming, but be diligent. The wisdom you will receive from it far outweighs anything else you could attain in this life.

purposed

Notes:

Prayers

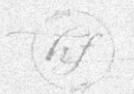

Whatcha Doin'?

By Larissa Bell

*But seek ye first the kingdom of God, and his righteousness;
and all these things shall be added unto you.*

Matthew 6:33

I read a devotional book in my early 20s about Moses. Several thoughts have stuck with me ever since. The author described the story of Moses fleeing Egypt and becoming a shepherd for many years — learning the ins and outs of feeding and caring for a large flock of sheep. Moses was getting training for leading the children of Israel in the wilderness while living his daily life. He was flexible to do whatever God wanted him to do because he was not tied down to the world.

The first point I learned was this — so many times in my teen and young adult years, I was focused on "I can't wait until I'm ___ years old because then I can do ___." I didn't realize the importance of using those years to prepare for God's adult plan for my life. Sure, I knew the information learned in high school and that becoming an EMT would help me have the knowledge needed for college and nursing school. But I can't ever remember thinking that using my young brain to become

Moses was flexible to do whatever God wanted him to do...

proficient in Spanish or being more diligent to practice my piano skills would allow me to serve the Lord better as an adult (when it's not so easy to learn those skills!). With mobile apps, YouTube, and library programs, it is not hard at all to find the resources needed to learn a language or instrument, tips on public speaking (for teaching Sunday School or speaking at a ladies' mission), computer skills (graphic design of bus or other ministry fliers or working in a church office), or first aid/babysitting skills (to be a godly influence in a daycare or children's ministry). The opportunities are more available now than ever before. So "whatcha doin'" to be the most prepared and ready Christian for whatever God has planned for you? (I Timothy 4:12-16)

The second point was just as impactful. There are many decisions teens and young adults make that could affect the rest of their lives. Choices regarding purity, substance use, and food intake and obesity can greatly affect your physical, mental, and spiritual health, which can limit your ability to wholly serve the Lord. Likewise, choices about where you work, college and career choices, hefty student loans, car payments, mortgages, etc. can affect you financially for many years and limit your freedom to be readily available for serving the Lord in the capacity God desires of you. Remember the rich young ruler in Mark 10? He "went away grieved: for he had great possessions" (vs. 17-25). I never want it to be said of me that I was so connected to my things or this world that I am not able to serve the Lord! (Matthew 6:33)

I am in my 40s now, but I still think about these two points frequently: what choices am I making that affect my ability to serve the Lord physically and whole-heartedly both right now and in the future, and am I making choices that tie me down to this world or allow me to be available to move when God speaks?

Challenge: I challenge you to critically think about how you spend your time. Is it on your own desires or things of this world? Or is it on how you can better serve the Lord with your mind, body, and soul right now and in the years to come?

purposed

Notes:

Prayers

The First Influencer

By Hope Reimers

In all thy ways acknowledge him, and he shall direct thy paths.

Proverbs 3:6

If you've been on social media for almost any length of time, you would easily find it is full of influencers. People who have gained an audience or following have influenced others to purchase a product, participate in a challenge, donate to a cause, or make decisions to better themselves. Smart influencers have a niche, which means their content is focused on one particular topic and is meant to reach a specific group of people. They will put much of their effort into extending that reach to as many people as possible. Not everyone who sees their content will follow them, but the more people see it, the more influence they gain. Influencers are at the mercy of algorithms. Their content will either go viral or flop depending on how many people view and react to it. Successful influencers know that it takes planning, preparation, consistency, and creativity to stay relevant to the public. It makes me wonder who started this entire idea. Not all influence is wholly good or bad, but it has proven to be extremely effective since the very beginning.

Allow God to be your biggest influencer for the day.

hf

Read Genesis 3:1-6. We see Satan was extremely influential in Eve's decision to eat the forbidden fruit. He offered Eve a perspective she had never heard before presented in a very positive way. The Devil wrapped this idea in a way that made it appear she was making the best choice possible for her well-being, but she learned the hard way that good intentions do not equal good decisions.

The Devil's niche is twisting the truth. His focus group of people to reach are Christians, and in this particular story, Christian women. He still continues to put all his effort into reaching as many people as he can. Ephesians 4:27 warns us to, "Neither give place to the devil." Not everyone who sees his twisted truths will follow or believe them. But the more people see them, the more influence he gains, whether they realize it or not. The Devil's influence is at the mercy of people who believe his ideas and spread them. His content will either go viral or flop depending on how many people view and react to it.

He knows that it takes planning, preparation, consistency, and creativity to infiltrate the minds of Christians, but he is an expert at it. The more people talk about his ideas, the more relevant he is to the public. Most influencers will take full credit for the success achieved through their work, but Satan's strategy is unique. He will gladly watch the effects of his ideas impact the lives and decisions of people, then he'll give those people someone or something to blame for the trials they face.

Satan stays in the shadows continuing to be a subtle, effective influencer while watching Christians point fingers at each other as a result. He is skilled at making his thoughts sound like our own and knows how to make us react to those thoughts just like he did with Eve. If he was able to convince the most perfect woman ever created, we can't ever think we're immune to his influence. He knew how to impact Eve's thoughts through his words and her eyes and is still using that same tactic today. Be fully aware of who truly impacts your decisions, whether it be through social media, books, shows, movies, or friends. There are many well-meaning people out there, but remember, good intentions do not always equal wise decisions.

Take Proverbs 3:6 to heart. See just how much of your life is impacted by acknowledging Him in every decision you make from the moment you stand up from this spot to the end of your day. Allow God to be your biggest influencer for the day.

purposed

Notes:

Prayers

When Is the Right Time to Speak?

By Candance Voyles

Open rebuke is better than secret love. Faithful are the wounds of a friend; but the kisses of an enemy are deceitful.

Proverbs 27:5-6

There is something we tell little girls – "Don't be a tattletale!" Children love to tell on others. Many times we have to direct them on what should be told or not. As we mature and come to know the Lord as our Saviour, those little girl relationships change, but one thing will remain the same – we will see others do things that they shouldn't do.

Life always has a way of becoming more complicated as we get older. It's not always easy to know how to handle situations in the right way. There is an accountability involved in friendship as we see in our verse. Many Christian young people struggle with the concept of when to be vocal when they see a peer headed down a wrong path. How do I know what to do, or should I just stay out of it? Even adults who have been saved for a long time still struggle with that concept. As God's children, we are accountable to truth and to the Spirit of truth that lives in us. If we truly love our friend we would never let them destroy themselves.

How do we handle it Biblically? We go to them personally. This isn't easy, but this is where being a Christian is really tested – not in the times of least resistance, but in the times where it may cost us something – even a friendship. If our friend won't listen or maybe if we aren't able to go to this peer, we go to the right person in leadership for guidance, maybe our parents or pastor. One thing we never do is go to other peers and discuss the matter. Then it becomes gossip and not true concern over our friend. It creates more damage. It becomes part of the problem and not the solution.

Many young people never want to involve an adult for fear of getting their friend in trouble or causing problems. Sadly, because of this, many young people have gone down a path of destruction, because no one cared enough to put up the proper road blocks. So when is the right time to speak? Just as when we were children, when we know something is going to hurt someone, even from a spiritual perspective, we speak. Sin destroys. Therefore, out of a heart of humility, knowing that we also are susceptible to temptation, we say something! We pray for boldness to stand and speak the truth in love. When we keep silent and let bad things happen, we're actually being complicit even though we weren't involved. We're not blameless in the situation when we know and could have given warning. James 5:20 says, "Let him know, that he which converteth the sinner from the error of his way, shall save a soul from death, and shall hide a multitude of sins."

purposed

Notes:

Prayers

Preparing for Marriage

By Rikki Beth Poindexter

As for me, I will behold thy face in righteousness:
I shall be satisfied, when I awake, with thy likeness.

Psalm 17:15

I love being married! I love talking to young women about marriage. I believe there are a few things that will greatly help as you are in this special season (whether single or in a relationship). Don't rush it!

Be teachable and remain that way. This is sadly becoming a lost art in the church. So many folks, young and old alike, think they have it all figured out (or they behave as if they do). Proverbs 12:1, "Whoso loveth instruction loveth knowledge: but he that hateth reproof is brutish."

Enjoy the season you are in. Do not spend so much time looking forward to the next season that you miss this blessed time. Clap and cheer for your friends who get married before you. I am amazed at those who cannot be happy for others as they wait. How silly! Ecclesiastes 3:1, "To every thing there is a season, and a time to every purpose under the heaven."

Have your own faithful and consistent walk with the Lord. How can you follow a man when you cannot follow the Father? For a marriage to

Have your own faithful and consistent walk with the Lord.

be successful, it will take two individuals walking consistently with the Lord. Do your best and do the work to get that quality time with the Lord every day. See it as necessary as your meals. Do you want the truth? It is more vital than your food. Psalms 119:10-11, "With my whole heart have I sought thee: O let me not wander from thy commandments. Thy word have I hid in mine heart, that I might not sin against thee."

Work on yourself. Strengthen or improve your relationships with your family and friends. Work on your education post-high school or get a job. Our great godly example of a wife and mother, the Proverbs 31 lady, was a working woman! If you are working, be the best employee. Find areas in your church where you can serve and be a blessing. Invest your time wisely before marriage. I Corinthians 7:32-33, "But I would have you without carefulness. He that is unmarried careth for the things that belong to the Lord, how he may please the Lord: But he that is married careth for the things that are of the world, how he may please his wife."

Save your money! Learn the discipline of saving. Have self-control.

Practice cooking. Pick out meals and shop for them. Ask questions. Ask other women for help or advice in the kitchen.

Learn how to fully clean a house from top to bottom.

Do some reading on the subject of becoming a wife. Ask your mom or pastor's wife for some recommendations. (I have plenty!) Watch other wives in your church. Learn what is pleasing to the Lord and what isn't. Talk to godly, older, wiser Christian women about the blessing of marriage.

Understand the concept of the five love languages. (This will help you so much. We feel loved in different ways, and we typically express love the way we feel loved.)

- Keep yourself pure.

- Guard your own heart (Proverbs 4:23).

- Control your thoughts. It is possible (Philippians 4:8)!

- Protect your body (I Corinthians 7:1).

- Pay attention to your clothes! Men are enticed and get excited about what they see. Do your part (I Timothy 2:9)!

Challenge: Never stop growing and learning! Strive daily to be more like the Savior. That is the best preparation for marriage. Read Psalms 17:15.

purposed

Notes:

Prayers

Iron Sharpeneth Iron

By Brittany Lindsay

Iron sharpeneth iron; so a man sharpeneth the countenance of his friend.

Proverbs 27:17

Friendship! Friendships are considered to be one of the most important aspects of a young person's life. Everyone wants to have friends and to be considered a friend. As Christians, friendship is also something that we must be so careful about. Friendships can be good for us (Proverbs 17:17), or friendships can be bad for us (Proverbs 13:20).

II Samuel 13:3-5 is a very good example of the influence friends have on us. Amnon had a friend, Jonadab. The Bible says that he was very "subtil" in verse three. "Subtil" means "crafty, cunning, sneaky, sly, and deceitful." He gave Amnon terrible advice in verse five. Jonadab was an enabler. Are some of your friends enablers (I Corinthians 15:33)? "Enable" means "to make able; to supply with power, physical or moral; to supply with means." Jonadab was supplying the thought, but never actually committing the sin. Be careful of what your friends are enabling you to do.

We can control what kind of friends we have and what kind of friends we are. These are some areas to guard ourselves in our friendships:

If they encourage you to lie to authority, they are not your friend. That may be your parents, pastor, etc. Jonadab told Amnon to lie to his authority in II Samuel 13:5.

If they encourage you to do wrong or help you sin, they are not a true friend. They are your enemy (Proverbs 1:10).

If they encourage you to think wrong about sin, like sin is not a big deal, they are not your friend.

If they make it easy for you to sin, they are not your friend.

If they have sin in their life, stay away. If you have a friend or friends that are okay with sin, it will affect you. One person is all it takes to wrongly influence your life (Proverbs 13:20).

Jonadab did not give Amnon the right advice, but he could have. He could have saved his friend's life from sin, but he didn't. Let's not be that kind of friend. We are to sharpen our friends. We cannot sharpen our friends unless we are sharpened ourselves. We must spend time with the Lord and keep sin out of our lives. We are to encourage our friends in the Lord and point them to Him. We have to work on our relationship with Him. Whether we realize it or not, we are an influence on others.

Looking back on my teenage years, I can see now that there were some friends that I should have removed from my life and some friends that I needed to hold dear. Take your friendships seriously. Friendships can shape your future. I've also thought, what kind of friend was I? Did I sharpen or dull my friend's countenance? Did I encourage that friend to love Jesus more, read their Bible and pray more, and serve Jesus with all their heart?

Challenge: Look at your own life. What kind of friend are you? How sharp are you? Are your friends sharpening you in the Lord?

purposed

Notes:

Prayers

Doest Thou Well to be Angry?

By Rebekah Miller

Then said the Lord, Doest thou well to be angry?

Jonah 4:4

It is impossible to hide a bad attitude from God. As we go about our days, there are many opportunities to become focused on our frustrations. There is a story in the Bible about a man named Jonah who also became focused on the ups and downs of life. God's response to this man can teach us how to handle the curves life might throw at us.

It is an understatement to say that Jonah had an attitude problem. We can see in Jonah 4:1, that Jonah was displeased and very angry that God showed mercy to the people of Nineveh. Only a little while ago, God showed Jonah that very same mercy when He saved Jonah from the belly of a big fish. While Jonah was upset, God asked Jonah, "Doest thou well to be angry?" Later in the chapter, God blessed Jonah with a gourd that withered the next morning. By midday, a wind had caused the sun to beat down on Jonah. The prophet became furious with the situation. God asks again, "Does thou well to be angry for the gourd?" Jonah vehemently replies, "I do well to be angry, even unto death"(Jonah 4:9). Jonah's anger over his situation may seem foolish to us, but how often do we become so focused on daily troubles that we allow ourselves to become bothered? Our response may not be the same as Jonah's response. Instead, we may roll our eyes when asked to do something or mumble under our breath when our plans get derailed.

As humans, our point of view is often consumed by the inconsequential things that we allow to creep in and irritate us, but God's point of view is perfect and just. While Jonah is lamenting the gourd, God offers us a peek into what he sees as important. In Jonah 4:10-11, God says, "Then said the Lord, Thou hast had pity on the gourd for which thou hast not labored, neither madest it grow; which came up in a night, and perished in a night: And should not I spare Nineveh...?" Every one of us can so easily become caught up with the temporal and forget to look at the world through God's eyes. Just as Jonah was concerned with his comfort over the souls of Nineveh, are we too busy looking at our troubles to consider those who need Christ?

purposed

Notes:

Prayers

Prepare Now for Marriage

By Andrea Leeder

Whoso findeth a wife findeth a good thing, and obtaineth favor of the Lord.

Proverbs 18:22

God's Word is the best place to start when preparing for marriage!

As a teen, I was excited at the thought of getting married one day. I always wanted to be a wife and mother. Here are some things I determined in my mind I would do to prepare to be a good wife.

First of all, I would have a walk with the Lord. If I was going to marry a godly man, I would need to be a godly young lady. You will attract what you are, so be the kind of person you want to attract.

I started reading my Bible through for the first time. I developed a prayer life. I took to heart messages I heard and tried to apply them to my life. I watched godly women who were serving God and had a good marriage.

Secondly, I learned how to cook. They say that the way to a man's heart is through his stomach (LOL!). I would help my mom cook and do dishes and clean the house.

Third, I tried to conduct myself properly. I tried to protect my testimony as a Christian young lady. I watched godly couples, pastors wives, and other godly single girls who were great examples.

Proverbs 12:4 says, "A virtuous woman is a crown to her husband: but she that maketh ashamed is as rottenness in his bones." I did not want to be a teen girl who was known for flirting or being loud around the guys. I wanted to act like a lady and make sure I was appropriate around boys. My parents taught us to have self-control. They also were wonderful examples of a good, godly marriage.

God's Word tells us how to act and conduct ourselves in such a way that we can be desirable to a young man. You need to spend time in His Word and read what the Bible says about being a virtuous woman.

I was determined as a teenager to work hard and take care of whatever it was the Lord entrusted to me – keeping things nice and tidy, babysitting, helping in the ministry, volunteering to do whatever needed done, etc. I was just trying to be a blessing, have a good attitude, and get along with people.

Challenge: I encourage you as a teen young lady to start thinking ahead about this subject of marriage and preparing yourself, not just to be a good wife but to be an excellent wife! Take a look at these verses for a good study on the virtuous woman, Proverbs 31:10-31.

"A virtuous woman is a crown to her husband:"
- Proverbs 12:4a

purposed

Notes:

Prayers

Drawing a Line

By Belinda Young

Take fast hold of instruction; let her not go: keep her; for she is thy life.

Proverbs 4:13

As a young person, you are under authority in every aspect of life. Someone tells you what you can do and what you can't do. Someone tells you what is right and what is wrong. Someone draws lines in your life between what is good and what is bad. These lines are drawn to protect you from being hurt and getting into sin and messing your life up.

But there comes a point in your life that you have to draw the lines. What are you going to do and why are you going to do it? What are you not going to do and why are you not going to do it? It will no longer be someone else telling you what to do, you will have to make an intentional effort to set a guideline that you can and will follow.

If you have taken heed to wise instruction, you can in turn make wise decisions to do the right things in your life – things you will not be sorry for.

Proverbs 4:13, "Take fast hold of instruction; let her not go: keep her; for she is thy life."

You may not have understood why you were not allowed to do certain things in your life, but as you grow and watch others make bad decisions, you begin to understand the "why."

Wisdom is obtained after you have heeded instruction – you turn around and understand why someone drew a line in your life.

Proverbs 4:7, "Wisdom is the principal thing; therefore get wisdom: and with all thy getting get understanding."

The Bible is of utmost importance as you mature and make decisions on things you will do and not do. The Bible will tell you truth and will keep your head level.

You can draw correct lines:

What will you wear?
What words will you say?
How will you say those words?
Who will you marry?
How will you conduct yourself before you are married?
How will you conduct yourself after you are married?
What will you listen to?
Who will you listen to?
What will your attitude be toward others?
What will your attitude be about yourself?
What will you do with your body?
What will you not allow your body to do?
How will you treat God and His Word?

To draw a line correctly, you must have the Word of God. When you draw the line, draw it tight and draw it straight. You will be tempted to go past that line.

Remember: You will have to take responsibility for your actions.

There is a young lady whom I love dearly – she has been saved for one year. She has on purpose made some decisions in her life.

Makenzi Hallman wrote – February 2023

Today marks one year of salvation by God's amazing grace. It may be a little late but after a little pondering, my New Year's resolution has been summed up to this one simple sentence. I want to be a brave woman for God! By brave, this is what mean...

B-BOLD. I want to stand up for my faith and honor Christ first and foremost even when it goes against the popular opinion.

R-RADICAL. I want to stand on the timeless Word of Truth and point others to Jesus even if that means it makes me a radically different girl. The truth will offend people. Jesus said so himself, but if I don't speak up for truth now, then when?

A-ANCHORED. I want my life to be anchored in the truth because God's Word never changes. Christians are called to be separated, we are not to keep up with worldly standards.

V-VIGILANT. I want to walk through this year with my eyes wide open. I want to be alert and looking for lies because our "adversary the devil, as a roaring lion, walketh about, seeking whom he may devour" 1 Peter 5:8.

E-EMPOWERED. I want to be empowered through God's Word, through the Holy Ghost and through truth – to step away when something goes against God's Word, not to be afraid of the consequences or what I may lose because I know living for Him is what I am called to do – not to please man but to please Christ alone. My purpose is to tell others of my Savior and to be all about Him.

61

This year I am choosing to be a BRAVE woman and not a wimpy woman. Biblical womanhood is sought after. It does not just come naturally! It is found on your knees in prayer! In 2023, my prayer is that Christ might be seen in me! There is no limit to God's love! He died for me and I want to live for him!

> The Bible will tell you truth and will keep your head level.

purposed

Notes:

Prayers

He's Done All Things Well

By Rainy Lehman

He hath done all things well:

Mark 7:37b

My preacher once said, "When you can't see where the Lord is, look at where He has been." I think it is safe to say we have all been in this place a time or two — when the world, the flesh, and the devil seem to be coming at you from every angle, and you do not understand what is going on. You are trying to do your best to pray, read your Bible, and do right, but you still seem to struggle. You know the Lord has not forsaken you because He promised that He wouldn't. At the same time, you just can't seem to find Him in the midst of your trial. It is during these times that I cling to this small, yet powerful, phrase in Mark 7:37, "He hath done all things well"!

While the context of this verse is speaking of people rejoicing as Jesus performed miracles, to me it is a reminder that there is nothing too hard for my God. He knows exactly where we are, the things we need, and the things we struggle with. When life is not going exactly as I would like or by my schedule, I can stand firm on the fact that "He hath done all things well." The Lord has never disappointed me and has never not had my best interest at heart.

What are you struggling with today? In your life, what may seem small and insignificant to others but consumes your every thought? When you start to feel overwhelmed, take the time to write down all the times in the past that the Lord has come through for you – every time He has answered a prayer, every time He has financially provided for you, etc. How about the day that He saved your soul from hell? Or the times He made Himself so real to you during your devotions? When you start looking back at all the many things He has done for you, you will quickly be reminded that He hath done all things well, and this time will not be any different!

Challenge: Go back to a time when you were struggling with something spiritually. Did God take care of you? Write down some blessings you have seen Him work through in your life. Remember, "He hath done all things well."

purposed

Notes:

Prayers

When God Says, "NO!"

By Sarah Russell

And the man of God answered, The LORD is able to give thee much more than this.

II Chronicles 25:9b

I have been a follower of Jesus Christ for many years. I am thirty-one years old and have been saved for twenty-three of those years. In my walk with the Lord, I have received many answers from Him. Many times the Lord has answered with a wonderful, "YES!" Sometimes, He answers with, "Wait, my child." I must admit, that's not my favorite answer. But the answer I disliked the most (in the moment) was my Lord's very clear "No."

I have received many "no" answers in my life. No, you don't need to take that job. No, this isn't the right path for you. And like a child, at times, I pouted and on occasion complained. The wrong attitude? Absolutely. I'm being transparent here. I was once a teenager too. I've failed as a Christian and at times strayed from the "yes" path just to take a small peak at the "no" road. But I must tell you, the "yes" path has always been lined with grace and goodness! While the "no" road has always been paved in hardness and regret.

One of the most significant no's I received in my early 20s was when I was seeking God's will about a young man who had shown interest in having a relationship with me. He was a godly young man by every estimation – respectful, serving in ministry.

But God said, "NO!" How could He object?! It was upsetting! I am truly going to be single for the rest of my life! This isn't fair. In my frustration, I cried to my Mother, "I'm so tired of God telling me no! I just want a yes!" Sounds a little familiar maybe? But I stopped complaining and stayed faithful to read and pray through this season. The Lord had said no. But He had given a promise with the no. He spoke to me through II Chronicles 25:9b, "The Lord is able to give thee much more than this." Much more than this? How could it be possible? I didn't know. But I repeated it to myself for every no: "The Lord is able to give thee much more than this."

And He did. Just one year later, I saw my husband for the very first time. As I write this, I am married to a handsome, loving man, who is a preacher of the gospel. I have three beautiful daughters, a family, great friends, and a home – a life full of peace and contentment like I've never known before! You see, when you choose to trust God and say, "Yes sir, my King! Your answer is no, and I am your obedient servant. Whatever you say! Lead me, sweet Saviour in the right and good way!" – you will never regret it.

Are you going through a no season right now? How is your attitude? Are you being submissive to your King?

Remember, "He is able to give thee much more than this," and He is always only good. He has great things in store for you! Stay faithful, my friend!

purposed

Notes:

Prayers

The Choice Is Yours

By Brittany Thompson

Woe unto them that call evil good, and good evil; that put darkness for light, and light for darkness, that put bitter for sweet, and sweet for bitter!

Isaiah 5:20

Growing up in a pastor's home, we listened to Patch the Pirate quite often. On one of the CDs, there is a song called "Bitter to Better." The chorus talks about how to turn bitter to better by one little letter and turning the "i" into an "e." We lived in Mexico for a period of time. We loved it. My childhood memories from there were so fun. I thought we'd live there forever, but that wasn't God's plan.

My grandpa pastored a church, but he became ill and passed away. The church voted my dad in as pastor. I couldn't believe it! Goodbye, Mexico. Hello, United States. I was young and confused at all that was happening. Saying goodbye to all that I was familiar with was hard to do. We moved to the States. It was God's will, but it was hard to adjust. It was difficult to get back to the culture. During the first few months of being back in America, I let myself get bitter. I missed my old friends; I missed simply everything. I hated when a member would talk to my parents about my misbehavior in church. I saw how coming and taking over a church here kept my parents quite busy. I was mad at God. I tried to fake happiness at church, but I was miserable during that process.

During our transition, the church was very gracious and kind to us. They went out of their way to spoil us and try to connect with us and love on us. It was after a message during Teen Connection that I realized being bitter isn't worth it. God moved in my heart that night. What a weight lifted off! We may not understand why God puts a new surprise in our life, but it's sweeter to trust in Him than getting angry and bitter.

Bitterness only hurts you. When I was hurting, I hurt others. What I was dwelling on and thinking about wasn't uplifting. I missed out on good memories because of my spirit in those first few months, but I'm so thankful now that God moved in my heart that day. Although life can come with surprises or changes in our circumstances, we can choose our attitude with it. What attitude will you decide? Search your heart to see if you have any bitterness toward God in any area.

It's sweeter to trust in Him than to get angry and bitter.

purposed

Notes:

Prayers

Friendliness = Friends

By Julie Payne

A man that hath friends must shew himself friendly:
and there is a friend that sticketh closer than a brother.

Proverbs 18:24

It's such a joy to have someone we can turn to, confide in, ask advice from, or just fellowship with! A friend! "Friend" means "one attached to another by affection." It further means your respect and affection for another leads to your desire for their company, and seek to promote their happiness and prosperity. Wow, what a loaded definition! Have you known someone who has never met a stranger and has a friendly smile for whoever they may meet? That is actually a very biblical way to be. Our verse from Proverbs 18:24 tells us that if we are to have friends, then we must be friendly! Friendly means "having the disposition of a friend; to promote the good of another."

Let's break it down:

- "A man" – This is you!
- "that hath friends" – This is what you want.
- "must shew himself friendly" – This is what you must be in order to get what you want. And let's remember the meaning of "friendly!" To be friendly, we are putting others above ourselves.

Your friends today are a result of your past friendliness!

- "and there is a friend that sticketh closer than a brother." – This is the promise from God if you do your part!

Now, think about this verse in your present state: "hath friends." Do you currently have friends (ones attached to you by affection – ones that desire your company and seek to promote your happiness and prosperity?), or do you sometimes feel friendless? It could even be "middle ground" where they are sometimes your friend, and sometimes not.

Next, let's think about "must shew." How has your friendliness in the past been. Your friends today are a result of your past friendliness.

Do you feel content with your friends, or do you wish you had more? Do you need to change your present state? This verse is not a "one chance at it and you're done" verse...NO! So think about this verse as a do-over. "Hath friends" can also imply to the future. Having more friends, though, means you going out there and being friendly right now. Your future friends are the result of your present friendliness.

You must also realize that even though you are obeying this verse, the other person, the friend, must also be obeying it. It takes both people being friendly to form a true friendship with each other, and that is the only way that friendship can last.

On a personal note, I admit I am not naturally a friendly person – meaning, since I have a shyer nature and an "in the background" personality, I have the opposite of an outgoing, bubbly personality that makes it easier (oh, I can imagine so much easier) to show friendliness!

But we of the shyer nature are not without hope. We can still show ourselves friendly even if we have to work a little harder at it. The Lord will not give us a command and leave us without a way to achieve it.

When I was a young teenager, I met a girl who was so friendly, not only to me, but to everyone else around as well. She made a great impression on me. So when I saw her again the next year, our friendship picked up right where it left off. Why? Because she showed herself friendly. I saw she was "true-blue!" Not a "friend" to one while back-biting another. She is what I think of when I read Proverbs 18:24, and her example is what helps me at times overcome my personality to be more friendly. This has been a tool the Lord has provided me to be able to achieve His command.

Here are some questions to challenge yourself with this verse. Are you a true friend? Do you show friendliness to everyone you see? What is your tool to help you in obeying this verse if you're the type of person that needs the extra help?

If you are naturally friendly, are you using your gift correctly? Or are you friendly to select ones while unfriendly to others? Please beware of this; people all around you can see this and you will soon be labeled as an unfriendly back-biter.

Read more verses on this subject for further study – Exodus 33:11; Ruth 2:13; Psalms 35:14; Proverbs 16:28; Proverbs 17:17, 27:6, 9-10, 17; John 15:13-15; Acts 27:3.

Determine to work on living out the definitions of these two key words! Friendliness = Friends? Yes!

purposed

Notes:

Prayers

The Chase of the Magical Pegasus Fairy Unicorn

By Christy Tadlock

If you love me, keep my commandments.
John 14:15

The steps of a good man are ordered by the Lord: and he delighteth in his way.
Psalms 37:23

God's will. The illustrious perfect magical hard-to-discern will of God. From having to figure out what person God wants you to marry for the rest of your life to figuring out what career God wants you to have. Oh, the stress! The anxiety!

Don't believe the lie of the devil. God's will is not some mystical truth playing hide-and-seek with you. God's will is simple. God wants you to know His will. How do I know that? Because He gave us a Bible full of His will.

God's will is for you to keep His commandments. If you love the Lord, keeping His commandments is the evidence of that love. The Bible is full of commands that are God's will.

For example:

- Be ye holy

- Keep thy heart will all diligence

- Forsake not the assembling of yourselves together

- Love the Lord thy God with all your heart, soul, and spirit

- Walk in the Spirit

- Be ye kind one to another

- Be ye steadfast, unmovable, always abounding in the work of the Lord.

And that's not even a fraction of what God tells us in black and white is His will.

God's will for you is to daily choose to follow Him. You must allow God to order your daily steps. Serving God doesn't happen magically. Walk in the light of His will that He has given you. If you are following God step-by-step for daily tasks, then trust and know that those step-by-step decisions are leading you straight into His will for those big decisions.

As young adults, so often we equate the question of "What is God's will?" with the question of "Whom will I marry?". These two questions are not the same. You must be actively living out the daily will of God that you do know (from the Bible) before you can confidently make any decisions about the person who is the will of God for you. Don't fret over God's will for your future; actively live out God's will for you today.

purposed

Notes:

Prayers

What Can I Do?

By Deborah South

Whether therefore ye eat, or drink or whatsoever ye do, do all to the glory of God.

I Corinthians 10:31

She was just a girl, carried captive from her homeland, afraid of the strange people, sights, and smells all around her in this foreign land. What could she do? Mrs. Naaman always had chores for her. When the girl found out that her master, Naaman, had leprosy, she did not hesitate to be a witness of the power of the God of Israel. II Kings 5:3, "And she said unto her mistress, Would God my lord were with the prophet that is in Samaria! for he would recover him of his leprosy." (Read II Kings 5:1-15.)

She was just a girl. What could she do? Her mother needed her to obey and to watch her baby brother in a basket in the Nile River. If he cried out, it could mean death for him. Oh, how she must have prayed as she watched the Egyptian princess take him from the water and sooth his cries. Miriam ran to offer the services of a Hebrew "nurse" for little Moses. (Read Exodus 2:4-8.)

She was just a girl. The people of the church were under much persecution. Their friend, Peter, had been put in prison for preaching the Word of God. Everyone was praying for the Lord to spare his life and release him. What could she do? She answered the door to see the Apostle Peter standing there alive! God had answered prayer! She ran to tell the others the good news even though they did not believe her testimony! (Read Acts 12:1-17.)

In these accounts, we see young girls doing simple tasks to help others. They were servants. They were obedient. Many times, I see young girls doing nothing. They feel they are too young to do anything for God or for others – or they are too busy doing what they want to do.

You are never too young to do a job for the Lord, to help others, or to be obedient!

Don't miss so much in life by dwelling in the future. "If I was 12, I would _____." "I wish I was 13, then I could_____." "When I turn 16, I will_____." "One day I will be 18 and then_____." You "wish" away your life while you could be doing so much now! You could be used of God now!

As a young person, you have more time to be a help to others. Here are some ways that you can be a blessing to others:

Be obedient! Bless your parents by obeying! People will respect you when you are doing right.

Be a testimony! You may be the only testimony that someone listens to. Young people have brought their friends to know Jesus just by asking them if they are saved. There is no age limit to witnessing for the Lord!

Draw a picture or send a card to someone who is sick, shut-in, or discouraged. Think of ways to encourage.

Offer to help someone.

purposed

Notes:

Prayers

Approve Excellent Things

By Lydia L. Riley

That ye may approve things that are excellent;
that ye may be sincere and without offence till the day of Christ.

Philippians 1:10

I love God's Word! I love how even when reading it for nearly all of my life, a verse can seem to literally jump off the page; so relevant, so alive, so full of truth, as if I had never seen that thought before! This little Scripture could change our lives if we focus on these three simple thoughts: approve excellent things only, be sincere, and be without offense until Jesus comes!

How often do we place our approval on things that God has no interest in? As teenagers especially, it can seem difficult to "stand out" or be the "odd-ball." It can seem so much easier to just go along with the crowd – maybe laugh at that off-color joke, not defend someone being made fun of, or simply never take a clear stand for righteousness when with the "cool kids."

What do you place your approval on? Sometimes not saying anything when something is going on that we know is wrong is actually putting our approval upon that situation or sin. Approve things that are excellent, Christian young lady!

Approve things that are excellent!

Excellent Manners. Our world is so rude. Don't fit into this mold! Read these verses about what God has to say about manners: I Corinthians 15:33, Ephesians 4:32, I Samuel 25:3. Be good. Be godly.

Excellent Morals. Live a life of sexual integrity and moral purity (Hebrews 13:4, I Corinthians 7:1-3). Be committed. Be consecrated.

Excellent Music. This area can really set a lady apart in our day. Look at Psalm 40:3. Our music can actually be seen by the world as a testimony! Music should honor Christ: Ephesians 5:19. Be Christlike. Be Conservative in the music you approve.

Excellent Media. We are inundated with worldliness and sin by movies, music, and social media. Make sure you draw the line tight and clean. If you can't honor Christ with it or watch or partake with Him right beside you and in you, then leave it alone. Read Romans 12:2. Is it good? Is it acceptable? Is it perfectly God's will for me? Don't ever put your approval on social media posts that are immodest, worldly, or posted by a rebellious teenager. I Corinthians 10:31, "Whether therefore ye eat, or drink, or whatsoever ye do, do all to the glory of God." Are my media choices for His glory or for my good?

Excellent Modesty. At the store, on vacation, in town, and at home, approve things that are excellent in your dress. There is a difference between the sexes. When pants on women first came into America, it used to be a shock (very similar to our day where now men are beginning to wear dresses). But eventually, constant exposure brings acceptance. Here are some verses to ponder: I Timothy 2:9, Deuteronomy 22:5, and Joshua 7:1, 21 (a hidden "goodly Babylonish garment" was part of the accursed thing and cost Achan his life and his family). Honor Christ in the way you dress in public and in private.

Excellent Ministry. God has a work for you to do! II Chronicles 31:20-21 – Do it with all your heart! The single years of your life can be given to the Lord in a very special way (I Corinthians 7:34). Be a servant of your church as Phebe was! In Romans 16:1-2, her church was her ministry! Find your place, minister from your heart. Devote your time and your talents to the work of God!

purposed

Notes:

Prayers

Anxiety or Peace?

By Breanna Patton

Be careful for nothing; but in every thing by prayer and supplication with thanksgiving let your requests be made known unto God. And the peace of God, which passeth all understanding, shall keep your hearts and minds through Christ Jesus.

Philippians 4:6-7

"Casting all your care upon him; for he careth for you" I Peter 5:7.

Anxiety can cause such turmoil in life, especially during the teen years. What if I told you that you do not have to struggle with anxiety? That you can give it all to God and He can and will give you a peace "which passeth all understanding?" God's Word tells us in Philippians 4:6-7, to "be careful for nothing." In other words, He is telling us to not worry and stress about things. What are you having anxiety about? School? Friends? College plans? Who or when you will marry? The future in general? I know that when I was a teenager and finishing high school, all of the things that I just listed were stressful and a burden to me. But it is possible to choose God's peace over anxiety.

How can you choose peace over anxiety? Trust in the fact that the Lord knows the future – the good, the bad, and everything in between. Jeremiah 29:11 tells us, "For I know the thoughts that I think toward you, saith the LORD, thoughts of peace, and not of evil, to give you an expected end." When I was a junior and senior in high school, I had anxiety about so many things, but as I went off to college, I claimed this verse knowing that the Lord knows all things and wants what is best for me. He wants what is best for you too! Therefore, I did not need to worry or fear. Of course, there were still times during those years when I allowed anxiety to rule and reign. However, any time the anxiety would come; I would always go back to Jeremiah 29:11, knowing that God was in control.

I wish that I had learned this lesson on choosing peace over anxiety sooner in my life. The Lord wants us to have peace all the time – through every trial, burden, and unknown of life. When that anxiety comes to the back of your mind, push it away and choose the peace of God. Life is so much more enjoyable when we allow God to be in control of the things that we cannot control.

Challenge: Find a verse that helps you overcome anxiety and memorize it. Quote it often when the anxiety comes.

purposed

Notes:

Prayers

Consequences of Criticism

By Alicia Moss

And Miriam and Aaron spake against Moses...

Numbers 12:1-16

Read Numbers 12, take heed to Miriam's actions, the Lord's response toward her, and the effects critical speech had on her and the people of God. Look at verse 1, "And Miriam and Aaron spake against Moses...." Miriam was guilty of criticizing her brother, the man of God, and Israel's leader. She did not agree with a personal decision made by Moses, therefore she thought so highly of herself that she verbally made her opinion known.

Refer to the ending of verse 8 and the beginning of verse 9: "wherefore then were ye not afraid to speak against my servant Moses? And the anger of the Lord was kindled against them...." The Lord spoke directly to Miriam, identifying the sin she had committed. God did not deal with her sin through confusion. He spoke directly to her. God left her with no question as to where she had wronged.

Lastly, verse 10 identifies the consequences of her sin, "...The cloud departed from off the tabernacle; and, behold, Miriam became leprous...." Although Miriam's words impacted her physically, they also impacted the church. During this time, the presence of God was felt and present through the cloud that led them. The Lord took His touch off of the church because of her words. Verse 15 states, "And Miriam was shut out from the camp seven days: and the people journeyed not till Miriam was brought in again." Due to Miriam's sin, she caused the church to become stagnate and be blocked from moving on for God.

How are your words today? Do you attack your man of God with your words? Does your tongue ooze words of negativity towards your pastor's wife, youth director, or those in leadership? God will not bless us or those around us when we criticize. Do you want to be the cause of your church losing the power of God?

Take heed and think before you speak. Don't be found guilty of criticizing those in leadership. Allow the Lord to work in your heart and ask Him to help you bridle a critical tongue.

Challenge: Write two effects of criticizing the man of God from Numbers 12.

1._____

2._____

Be honest with yourself, repent, and determine to keep your words off the man of God from this day forward!

purposed

Notes:

Prayers

What's That Smell?

By Renee Patton

Be not deceived: evil communications corrupt good manners.

I Corinthians 15:33

Have you walked into the kitchen and thought, "PEWWWW!" – only to find out it was one rotten potato that turned into five rotten potatoes?! Everything the bad potato touches is now corrupt also. Thus, our verse – say it out loud: "Be not deceived: evil communications corrupt good manners," I Corinthians 15:33.

Everything that touches me will affect me. People, whether it be friends or acquaintances, can make us stink! Our response to circumstances can make us stink. The Bible is clear that "...evil communications corrupt good manners," I Corinthians 15:33b.

Say this verse out loud again, "Be not deceived: evil communications corrupt good manners," I Corinthians 15:33. God wants us to get a grip and understand that others affect us. You cannot continually walk through life and be unaffected by evil communications. Evil communications can be bad speech, gossip, intimidation, anger, malice, unkindness, etc. When we submit ourselves to daily rotten potatoes, we are likely to become one!

"Be not deceived...." (I Corinthians 15:33a), do not kid yourself! If I allow the bad to rub off on me, I will be bad too. I, you, we all must walk circumspectly at things around us, so we may fight off the rotten potatoes around us! Say this verse again, "Be not deceived: evil communications corrupt good manners," I Corinthians 15:33.

We cannot allow others to affect what God has for us to do in this life. We must guard our hearts from evil communications so they will not corrupt us! Surrender your heart daily to the Lord and ask Him to help you make correct choices. Ask Him to keep those smelly, rotten potatoes away from you! Better yet, are you a smelly, rotten potato affecting others? If so, God will give you the strength to overcome this if you only ask Him!

Say this verse one more time for me, "Be not deceived: evil communications corrupt good manners," I Corinthians 15:33. The more we remember that evil communication will corrupt us, the better we are able to fight off the corruption and temptations brought daily to each of us. God wants us to succeed! I want you to succeed! Your Pastor wants you to succeed! Surrender your heart to God and ask Him to guard your heart. Ask God to show you evil communication so that you may be strong and fight off corruption! No one wants to be stinky! You are too precious to God to be a rotten potato!

Challenge: Memorize I Corinthians 15:33. Keep it close to your heart! God will remind you of it when you need it!

purposed

Notes:

Prayers

Working While You Wait

By Victoria Kiker

The Lord recompense thy work,
and a full reward be given thee of the LORD God of Israel,
under whose wings thou art come to trust.

Ruth 2:12

The book of Ruth has always been fascinating to me. It's a story of heartbreak and tragedy, loss and restoration, hardship and success – a love story. Really, what's not to enjoy?! It's a beautiful picture of God's grace and redemption.

One of the things that intrigues me most about Ruth is that she left everything she knew in Moab – her home, country, family, her life – to follow her mother-in-law into a foreign land. Ruth got to Bethlehem only to realize she wasn't much better off. She was still a widowed stranger with nothing of value, spending hours of hard labor to barely get by. Sounds quite depressing, doesn't it? But Ruth was doing what was required of her at that time. As Elizabeth Elliott would say, Ruth was willing to "do the next thing." I'm sure at the time she had no idea what her future looked like, but she remained faithful to "do the next thing."

Ruth's time in the field was a waiting period in her life. She was simply doing what had to be done. I'm sure the long days of waking early and staying late to glean in the fields were not the most enjoyable or easy, but she was faithful in her task. It was on one of those faithful days that she was noticed and introduced to Boaz. That day began the start of her life changing forever.

Many of us find ourselves in waiting periods of life. Not just as teens or young adults, but all throughout life there will be times when God has us wait. Fill in the blank: what are you waiting for? One of the best things you can do while you wait is work! What can you do while waiting for God to change your circumstance or give you direction? God honors those who, with a servant's heart, wait patiently.

If Ruth had whined about her current circumstances and refused to go to work that day, she may never have met Boaz. Her life may have turned out very differently. If she hadn't been determined to work while she waited, she may have never remarried or had a family of her own. Side note: Ruth became a part of the lineage of Jesus Christ (Matthew 1). What an honor she received! Would that have happened if she had refused to work while she waited? I don't know. But I know this, God honored her obedience and faithfulness.

Let me encourage you. I know that waiting is hard, but there are valuable lessons to learn while in waiting rooms. Pour your heart out to the Lord, let Him know you're willing to wait for His best, and in the meantime, work. Psalms 62:5 "My soul, wait thou only upon God; for my expectation is from him."

Challenge: Study Psalms 62:5. Look up "expectation" in Webster's 1828 dictionary. Search the word "wait" in scripture, especially in the book of Psalms.

purposed

Notes:

Prayers

Influencer

By Kate Ledbetter

*I beseech you therefore, brethren, by the mercies of God, that ye present your bodies
a living sacrifice, holy, acceptable unto God, which is your reasonable service.
And be not conformed to this world: but be ye transformed by the renewing of your mind,
that ye may prove what is that good, and acceptable, and perfect, will of God.*

Romans 12:1-2

Influence - To move by moral power; to act on and affect, as the mind or will, in persuading or dissuading; to induce. To lead or direct.

We live in a day where it is very popular to be an "influencer." People want to be someone who everyone else wants to be. The only problem is that everyone seems to want to be the same. The same looks, hairstyles, clothing, and carnality seem to reign among us. Even young Christian ladies are falling into the trap of social media content (what you post) being more important than being content (happy with who you are and what you have in Christ).

Maybe you have a platform that has drawn a crowd, and you feel the weights and pressures of that in your life. If so, let me ask you this, how are you influencing others? Does your platform just look like everyone else's? Do you share your everyday life but leave the Lord out of it? Are you afraid to be a Christian in the real world?

Romans 12:1-2 talks of presenting your body as a living sacrifice and not being conformed to this world. How transformed are you? When the world looks at you and what you represent, are you just like them or are you giving them something different? Are you trying to be the world's idea of "real" or are you actually real? Are you unafraid of standing up for the truth in a world that would rather have carbon copies who "live their truth"? Do people even know you claim to be a Christian? Have they heard your testimony or are you just giving them hair tutorials, clothing breakdowns, and decorating tips?

Challenge: Other young girls are watching you. Ask yourself: Does my life persuade them to be like everyone else or does it persuade them to be more like Christ? If the whole world were watching me, what influence would I have? Is my Christianity generic or authentic? Romans 15:14, "And I myself also am persuaded of you, my brethren, that ye also are full of goodness, filled with all knowledge, able also to admonish one another."

Young Christian ladies are falling into the trap of social media content being more important than being content in Christ.

purposed

Notes:

Prayers

What Can I Give Him?

By Hannah Suttle

For to their power, I bear record, yea, and beyond their power they were willing of themselves; Praying us with much intreaty that we would receive the gift, and take upon us the fellowship of the ministering to the saints. And this they did, not as we hoped, but first gave their own selves to the Lord, and unto us by the will of God.

II Corinthians 8:3-5

I grew up as a ministry kid. My dad was the youth pastor of a church in Virginia when I was born and became the pastor of the same church when I was four years old. When I was fourteen, we began deputation and two years later headed to Denmark as missionaries. As a kid in the ministry, you find that most of your friends' parents are in the ministry as well. I had a few friends close by that were pastors' daughters, but a lot were missionary kids! It didn't matter that we were miles apart and could only converse through letters and emails ... our lives were similar, and we just clicked.

As I entered into my teenage years, some of these friends started to grow apart. When they turned eighteen, a few left their homes and went fast and hard into the world. When I asked them why, more often than not, their answer was the same ... "My parents spent too much time at church and never really spent time with us." Bitter ministry kids? This was so hard for me to comprehend! Instead of viewing the ministry given to their parents as an opportunity to serve the Lord together and learn firsthand about how to better please Him, my friends were viewing the ministry as something that was stealing their parents away from them.

If you're a teenager who is struggling with these thoughts right now, I just want to encourage you to keep serving the Lord! God placed you in your home and family for a very specific purpose. As hard as it may be for you that your parents are away and ministering so much, it's hard for them to be away from you too! I want to encourage you to view this as something you can give to God instead of viewing it as a trial! God wants to bring you to the point where you are willing to give Him more than just tithes, offerings, and a few hours a week at church. He wants all of you!

I promise you, there is no greater joy than surrendering your all to God and watching what He can do with it! I want to encourage you to ask your parents for ways you can help them and get involved. As much as parents have to surrender their children to the Lord, children have to surrender their parents too! You will never regret surrendering your all to the Lord!

purposed

Notes:

Prayers

Love Made Me Do It!

By Kim Thompson

For this is the love of God, that we keep his commandments:
and his commandments are not grievous.

I John 5:3

Matthew 22:37 "Jesus said unto him, Thou shalt love the Lord thy God with all thy heart, and with all thy soul, and with all thy mind."

Teenagers, do you ever struggle with the standards and convictions of your parents, your pastor, or your church?

I was born into a Christian home; however, we didn't become independent Baptists until I was nine years old. Being that young, I didn't struggle at all with some of the changes that were taking place in our lives. I had no problem at all giving up pants for skirts. Do you know why? I loved my mother, and it gave me joy to please her.

By the time I reached my early teen years, I was highly aware of ... boys! During one particular summer moment as we strolled the mall, I thought, "Man, I feel stupid in this skirt!" It wasn't so much that I wanted to dress immodestly; it was that I wanted to fit in! I look back at that moment now, and I understand how crucial it was that I did the right thing! I could have gone home and announced to my mother that I was done dressing the way she wanted me to dress, and I would have hurt the one person in my life who had sacrificed the most for me – and for what? (At this point, my dad was in heaven, and Mom was on her own rearing us kids!) But do you know what made me go home and just "get over" that moment in the mall? Love! I loved my mother!

That love for my mother has transferred over the years to the Lord Jesus Christ! Now, I dress for Him, a righteous and holy God, and dressing right is not grievous because I love Him.

Teenagers, the next time someone cruel is wanting to make you feel weird since you have a modest outfit on, just kindly ask her: Have you ever been in love? (That question alone will change the dynamic of the situation.) If she responds, you can come back with any statement like this, "Since you've been in love, you know that pleasing that person is the thing that matters most to you! Modesty pleases the Person I love the most." Mic drop.

purposed

Notes:

Prayers

Integrity...
The Forgotten Guide

By Misty Wells

The integrity of the upright shall guide them:
but the perverseness of the transgressors shall destroy them.

Proverbs 11:3

Have you ever tried to reach a destination without a guide? Maybe someone tried to give you directions using landmarks, but you never reached the place you were longing to go because you didn't have a map. Being misplaced is a terrible feeling. Not knowing which way to turn or where to go can be discouraging. I've felt that way in my own life at times. Desiring God's will for my future but unsure how to get there. Wouldn't it be wonderful if we had a guide?

According to the King James Bible dictionary, a guide means "to lead or direct in a way; to conduct in a course or path; to guide a traveler who is not acquainted with the road or course." Ladies you are walking a path that you've never traveled before. You need a guide if you're going to make it to your destination. For those of you who are saved, I have great news! You have one and his name is Integrity.

Integrity in the Old Testament is " the condition of being without blemish, completeness, perfection, sincerity, soundness, uprightness, and wholeness." In the New Testament it means "honesty and adherence to a pattern of good works." If you're reading this devotional, I'm sure you're concerned about the direction of your life. You may be thinking about a husband, a family, or the ministry. All these things are honorable, but are you living a life of integrity first? Are you faithful in the "now" (Luke 16:10)? There are responsibilities at every stage of life. Be dependable in what you have been trusted with now. Do you have trouble controlling your spirit (Proverbs 25:28)? Bad attitudes are very unattractive. Learn to control yourself. What about your finances (Proverbs 13:16, 31:16)? Manage your spending now before the mortgage payment comes along. Learn to pay those bills on time. Are you living a life of integrity when no one is looking (Proverbs 15:3)? Pick up that piece of trash on the church pew. Give to that missionary without anyone knowing about it. Singing in our churches is needful and playing an instrument to the best of your ability is absolutely necessary, but these are not the attributes that will direct your path.

I have seen many doors open and others close by simply allowing integrity to guide me. The Lord does not intend to keep you guessing about His will for you. He has a beautiful destination for your life, and if you follow the guide, you will get there in His time.

purposed

Notes:

Prayers

Whom Do You Fear?

By Ashley Thompson

*Let us hear the conclusion of the whole matter: Fear God,
and keep his commandments: for this is the whole duty of man.*

Ecclesiastes 12:13

Fear God, and keep His commandments. Wow! That's an all-encompassing command. If everyone lived like that, we would live in a perfect world! If we truly feared God, we wouldn't have to be told to keep His commandments, we would just do it.

Now, fear is not talking about being afraid of God. I grew up with a fear of my Dad. Many times my fear of him kept me from doing wrong. I love my Dad! I'm not scared of him, but I greatly respect him. I knew that if I did something bad, chastisement would follow. At times I wasn't too worried about the chastisement, but it was knowing my wrong actions would hurt and disappoint him that kept me from doing wrong. To fear is to feel and show great reverence.

I read something in my devotions the other day that really jumped out at me. In Exodus 1, when Pharaoh tells the Hebrew midwives to kill the male babies, it says in verse 17, "But the midwives feared God ...."

Their fear of God was greater than their fear of Pharaoh, and it kept them from doing evil! God honored that, and in verse 21, we see He made them houses because they feared Him. Another thing that I thought was pretty neat is that He mentions two of the midwives by name: Shiphrah and Puah. These two women have their names permanently written in God's Word simply because they feared Him and did right. They're not given a whole chapter. We don't know anything about them outside of their occupation, but generations of people have read their names and what they did time and time again. God is not random. They're not mentioned by accident. Their fear of God mattered!

During these teen years, so many changes and decisions are made. The choices you are making today are creating the person you'll be tomorrow. Do you fear God or peer pressure? Who are you worried about pleasing? If it's not God, then I can tell you, you're headed for some serious hard-knocks. Psalms 31:19 says, "Oh how great is thy goodness, which thou hast laid up for them that fear thee ...." Do you want God's goodness and blessing on your life? Fear God, and keep His commandments, and the rest will fall into place!

The choices you are making today are creating the person you'll be tomorrow.

purposed

Notes:

Prayers

Tips for the Tough Times

By Marissa Patton

My heart is fixed, O God, my heart is fixed: I will sing and give praise.

Psalm 57:7

Fixed: to make stable; to set or establish immovably. Is your heart established in Christ? I mean, come on. It is hard to be set on anything during this season of your life, right? Your emotions are all over the place...laughing one minute and crying the next for "no reason." Your mind is probably overrun with your plans for the future. I wanted to pass along a few valuable tips for those overwheling times of sadness, confusion, uncertainty, or fear.

Stay close to the Lord. Keep up those daily devotions. Find a good reading plan or devotional. Write that prayer list. Keep a thankfulness or answered prayer journal. Do whatever it takes to stay spiritually connected to God. I used to write out my prayers to God when I was struggling. Do what works for you to keep your relationship strong in Him (Psalms 63:1).

Sit down with a godly lady. Chat late into the evening with your mom about your struggles. Reach out to your pastor's wife for some advice for navigating these years. Spend some time with godly influences like your Christian school teachers or ladies in ministry in your church. A lesson I learned too late was asking for tips and advice about life after high school. You will find that these words of wisdom will stick with you your whole life (Proverbs 11:14)!

Surround yourself with good friends. One bad friend can lead you down a path of sin so quickly. Watch out for negative peer pressure. Stay close to those girls that want to serve the Lord (Proverbs 27:17)!

Stay connected in your church. No matter how hard the struggles are, stay in church! Do not miss out on services or ministry opportunities just because you are having a bad day. Staying in church near God's people will encourage you in the Lord on the toughest days (Hebrews 10:25).

I hope these gave you some ideas of how to better navigate the hard days. Make sure to keep your heart open to what God wants to teach you. Keep your heart fixed on Him and His plan for your life!

purposed

Notes:

Prayers

Do You Know the Answer

Anonymous

*Let your speech be alway with grace, seasoned with salt,
that ye may know how ye ought to answer every man.*

Colossians 4:6

Ever come in contact with a bully? Or worse, someone who is your "friend" but constantly questions what you stand for? Believe it or not, even in a Christian school or good church there will be a "friend" who will make you feel self-conscious about a conviction in your life - your choice to be modest, listen to godly music, attend church regularly, hang out with godly influences, etc. If you are in a public school, those people who question you are multiplied.

My question is, "Do you know the answer?" When someone is asking about your convictions (with genuine interest or with evil intent) can you answer their questions according to the Bible? Why do you believe the way you believe? Why do you dress like that? Why do you attend church? Isn't your life boring with all those rules? You can answer them! You have God's Word on your side. I am sorry to say that I missed out on many opportunities to be a light in a dark world because I could not defend my beliefs like I should have been able to.

Take these years and learn all you can about what you believe. It will help you be a stronger Christian. It may even open the door for you to graciously share with others your beliefs from the Bible. "Study to shew thyself approved," says II Timothy 2:15. Below are a few topics you can study. Write the references down in your Bible as you find answers.

What does it mean to be saved?

Why do you dress modestly?

Why don't you watch certain movies or listen to worldly music?

Why do you go to church all the time?

Do your parents make you do (fill in the blank)?

Why are your parents so strict?

Why is the Bible so important?

You can be bold in your answers, knowing that God's Word backs up what you believe. Learn "how ye ought to answer every man."

purposed

Notes:

Prayers

Enjoy the Ride

By Grace Shiflett

And having food and raiment let us be therewith content.

1 Timothy 6:8

Content: to be strong, to suffice, to be enough

How many times have we heard preaching about contentment? Or been told to be content? This is for sure easier said than done. I believe we would all agree on how much better our daily lives would be if we would learn to be content.

Can I encourage you to learn to be content while you are still young? Don't spend your days wishing for the next latest and greatest. Embrace your moments of life and enjoy the ride. So many miss out on joy by wishing for the next day to come, the "perfect" age, more material things, a boyfriend, and the list goes on and on.

A majority of girls your age go through what could be some of the best days of their lives, but they miss it by not being content with food and raiment. There will always be highs and lows along the journey of your teen years (and your lifetime), but choose to be content with "such things as ye have" (Hebrews 13:5)!

If you don't learn to daily live choosing contentment, you will carry this ungrateful spirit into every stage of life. We all know people who live in continual discontentment: the person who thinks they will be happy if...fill in the blank. The sad part is that there is never an end to filling in the blank if contentment is not learned. It was a great day in my life when I began to make a conscious effort to learn contentment in my heart. Philippians 4:11, "Not that I speak in respect of want: for I have learned, in whatsoever state I am, therewith to be content."

Don't let your mind constantly wander, wanting something else or just not okay with the path God has laid for you. Trust in His process for your life! Your story is not over! Learn to be content and enjoy the ride.

purposed

Notes:

Prayers

About The Authors

Each author has been handpicked because of their Christian
testimony. God has gifted each writer with incredibly versatile
perspectives of the Christian life. These godly ladies come
from all walks of life including pastor's wives and daughters,
missionary wives, church staff ladies, and faithful church members.
Their written words of wisdom are sure to bless your heart.

To know more about our writers please visit:
thehighlyfavouredlife.com/our-story

Salvation Made Simple
By Renee Patton

Admit. One must first admit they are a sinner. Romans 3:10 states, "As it is written, There is none righteous, no, not one." Sin is everywhere and we all commit sin, many times without even trying. Perhaps in a conversation, we say something innocently, then realize it was not correct. That, my friend, is lying. Of course, murder is a sin that is seen and felt by those affected. However, lying is too. Jeremiah reminds one that "The heart is deceitful above all things, and desperately wicked: who can know it?" (17:9). A baby does not have to be told how to sin, it is simply in our nature. One must admit they are a sinner otherwise we make God a liar as found in I John 1:10, "If we say that we have not sinned, we make him a liar, and his word is not in us."

Believe. One must believe Jesus came to this earth to be born and die for our sins. "For God so loved the world, that he gave his only begotten Son, that whosoever believeth in him should not peish, but have everlasting life" (John 3:16). God desires that we should not perish, thus the choice is ours. God gives man the opportunity for salvation if man would take it. Romans 5:8 states "But God commendeth his love toward us, in that, while we were yet sinners, Christ died for us." Webster's 1828 Dictionary defines commendeth as entrusts or gives. So, God gave us His love through His Son, Jesus. Furthermore, Romans 5:19 shows how sin came from Adam and is made righteous through Christ, "For as by one man's disobedience [Adam] many were made sinners [mankind], so by the obedience of one [Jesus] shall many [mankind] be made righteous."

Confess. Confession is made with one's own mouth. The words must come from the person alone. Romans 10:9 talks of both confession and believing, "That if thou shalt confess with thy mouth the lord Jesus, and shalt believe in thine heart that God hath raised him from the dead, thou shalt be saved." The key is I have to confess to God. My husband or friend cannot confess for me. While God gives man the opportunity on earth, there will be a time every knee will bow and confess God is Lord, "For it is written, As I live, saith the Lord, every knee shall bow to me, and every tongue shall confess to God" (Romans 14:11).

To see more resources on salvation visit:
https://www.thehighlyfavouredlife.com/simple-salvation

If you made this decision, please contact us at *highlyfavouredlife @gmail.com.* We would love to rejoice with you in the new life you now have in Christ.

prayer

A Highly Favoured Life Devotional

Check Out
The Highly Favoured Life
on

and
thehighlyfavouredlife.com

www.ingramcontent.com/pod-product-compliance
Lightning Source LLC
Chambersburg PA
CBHW060324050426

42449CB00011B/2635